My Christian Counseling Companion

Also written by Kimberlee Herman

Women of the Bible
Wise Parenting: Guidelines from the Book of Proverbs

MY

COUNSELING
COMPANION

SPIRITUAL TOOLS AND REFLECTIVE QUESTIONS
TO SUPPORT YOU ON YOUR COUNSELING JOURNEY

KIMBERLEE HERMAN, MSW, LCPC

AZAR PRESS

Azar Press is a product of Redeemed Hope
www.RedeemedHopeAz.com

Revised edition

A special thank you to all my clients over the years who have inspired me with their bravery as they entered into counseling for the first time.

Thank you, God, for the pivot in my career to focus on teaching clients how to turn to you for your guidance, love, and healing. You are the Wise Counselor and your guidance is always best.

A huge thank you to Dave (my husband) and Madison (our daughter), for their unending encouragement.

Thank you to my graphic design consultant, Karen Dahlquist (www.HappyFish.com). I am not an artist, but I pretend to be in my books (ha!) and need all the help I can get. I am a watercolor fan and if I could really paint, this is how my journal would look. I hope you like it.

May we all seek God deeply for His healing and His glory to shine through us in this sacred work we call counseling.

This page left intentionally blank

TABLE OF Contents

Welcome.

I'm so glad you are here.

After nineteen years in this sacred line of work, I realized that having a resource for my clients to keep organized with their counseling journey could be super helpful. Plus, there is little time in session to teach spiritual disciplines. These disciplines can be a nice boost to nurturing your relationship with God.

Over my career, the one conclusion I have for you is this: Moving towards God is the **most** essential part of your healing process.

God is hope. God is love. God heals. Without inviting Him into your counseling, all you have is mankind's invention of psychological theory. While that is okay (and helpful), God's spiritual help is **crucial**.

Cultivating this relationship with God can be accomplished in many ways. This journal outlines 10 different spiritual disciplines to try out and incorporate into your life.

In your counseling sessions, seeds of change will be planted. However, you will grow and heal faster if you take the time to nourish those seeds **between** sessions.

Working on yourself is like stepping into **Mark 12:31** which tells us to love our neighbors as ourselves (paraphrased). This means we can't love others well until we love (care for) ourselves first.

Who is This Journal For?

This is for the woman who is entering or currently in counseling.

You do not need to be in Christian counseling nor be a Christian to use this journal. It is, however, focused on teaching Christian spiritual disciplines to grow in faith and draw closer to God.

What is the Purpose?

This journal is a guide to enhance and support you between your counseling sessions. It is to help you keep organized with your questions, feelings, and growth.

Having a foundational relationship with God is key especially as you renew your mind with the truth of God. Sometimes this takes place in counseling, but most of the time it will be between sessions and is up to you to make that happen. This journal will help guide you with that progression.

Using **My Christian Counseling Companion** can also help you process and apply what you learned in counseling by answering the reflection questions after each session as well as taking the time to fill in the journaling pages with your thoughts, prayers, and praises.

Disclaimer

This journal is a support tool for you as you work with your own counselor. This is not meant to replace any professional counseling.

The spiritual disciplines laid out in this journal are practical ways to connect to God. Reading your Bible is always the best place to start, but sometimes using different approaches can make the connection deeper or just different.

The resources in this book are meant to be a source of helpful suggestions. It's okay if you prefer some over others. It is also okay if you do not want to use all of them. Use what works for you. In addition, web pages and apps change over time. So the resources listed in the back may not be available at some point in the future.

For those that may feel suicidal, you can call or text the national suicide hotline at: 988 (yes, just 3 numbers) as well as your counselor.

For those that would like prayer, you can call the 700 club hotline at 1-800-700-7000 or HIS prayer line at 866-987-7729.

How to Use This Journal

- This journal is meant to go through slowly. Read only one chapter as often as you have a counseling session.

- Try memorizing the scripture that starts each chapter.

- Read the spiritual disciplines and try them out.

- *Before* each counseling session, spend time thinking about what you want to cover. Jot down your ideas under "Topics to discuss."

- Soon after your session is over, write out your takeaways.

- Write down any homework your counselor gave to you.

- Take time to answer the self-reflection questions.

- The blank pages between sessions are for you to journal (or draw) thoughts, questions, etc. Use the feelings wheel on page 7 as needed. You can choose to share this with your counselor or keep it to yourself. If you really like to write, I have created a matching journal you can use.

- This book is set up for 10 sessions of counseling. You may not need all 10 or you might need more, in which case you can purchase a second journal or follow the format on your own.

- Or use this book how it fits you best.

Let's get started!

What if Counseling is
Not Working?

When you start counseling, you will be asked about your goals. In essence, what do you want to work on to make your life better or more manageable?

Sometimes life happens and those goals are pushed to the side so you can work on more urgent issues. This is common.

If, for whatever reason, your counselor is not focusing on what you need or starts talking about their lives or struggles too much, it may be time to end working with that person and start with someone new.

Counselors can share a bit of their story if it helps your situation or brings more revelation to your struggle. I have heard over the years of some counselors becoming friends with their clients by sharing their burdens and asking for advice instead of being the listener. This is not okay as it creates confusion and blurs the lines of the relationship roles.

Not all counselors use the same counseling methods. Some counselors are there to help you process life. Some use healing methods, some specialize, and others don't.

If you are open with your counselor but are not feeling heard or helped after 3-4 sessions, then it may be time to look for someone new (websites to find someone new are under "resources" on page 92). Check out their website. Is it professional and clear? Then pray. Pray that you are led to the right person who will help you.

Let all that I am wait quietly before God, for my hope is in him. He alone is my rock and my salvation, my fortress where I will not be shaken.

- Psalm 62:5-6

Practical use of the Feelings Wheel

Using a feelings wheel can help pinpoint emotions.

Sometimes we feel hate when really deep down we are jealous. Or we feel scared when deep down we are overwhelmed. We can even be upset at someone and realize it is because we are confused about how they are treating us such as when dealing with someone's narcissistic behaviors.

When we have emotions it is important not to ignore them. Sometimes it is best to journal or draw what is going on and discuss with your counselor. Use the blank pages in this journal to support that action.

Other times you can use some outlets to release your feelings such as:

- exercise to discharge the extra energy inside
- throw some punches at a punching bag or pillow
- talk to God about some sadness
- write out your anger, then rip it up and throw away
- read scripture to comfort you

Ask your counselor for some ideas for you as well.

Feelings Wheel

Use the Feelings Wheel to help identify emotions

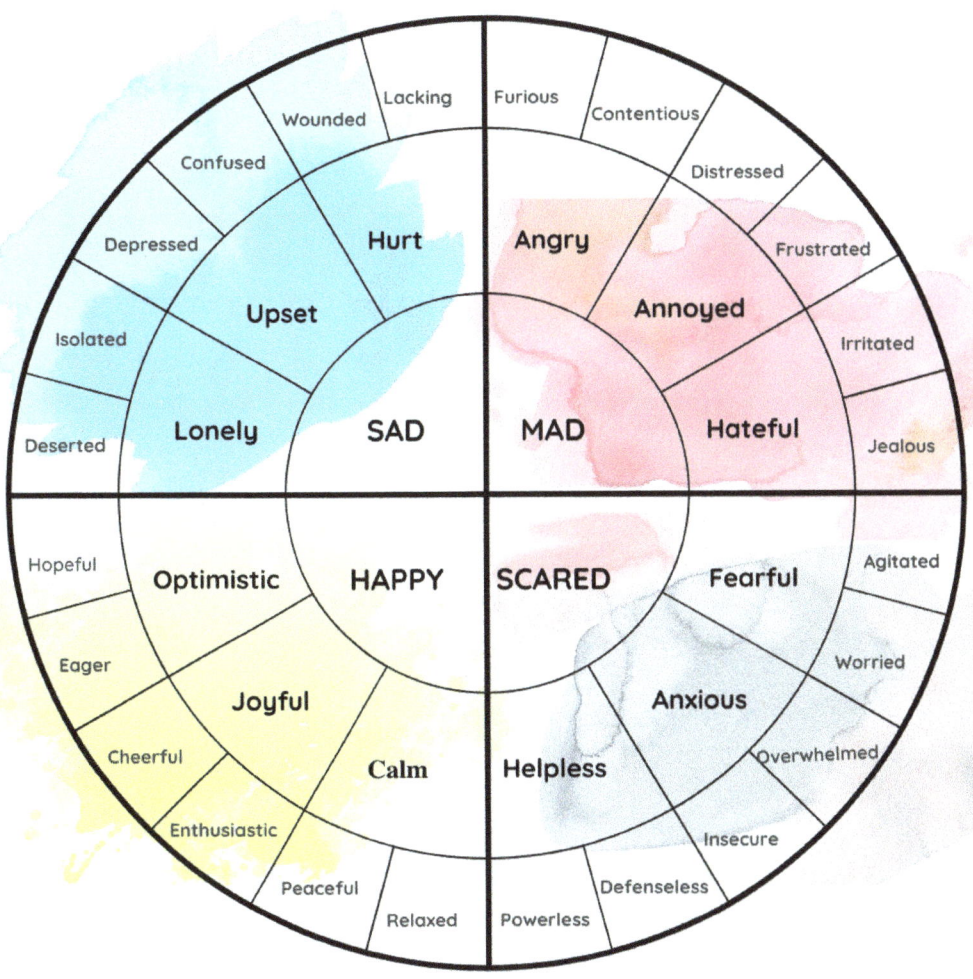

Initial Self-Reflection Questions

What are my expectations going into counseling?

....

....

....

....

....

What are my thoughts like (list positive and negative)?

....

....

....

....

....

How will I know that change has occurred?

....

....

....

....

What does my relationship with God look like?

....

....

One

Don't be afraid, for I am with you.
Don't be discouraged, for I am your God. I
will strengthen you and help you. I will hold
you up with my victorious right hand.

-Isaiah 41:10

Spiritual Discipline #1

Let's Make It Personal

The Bible is full of encouraging words and direction. However, it can often feel like it is not personal to us, right? **Personalizing scripture** helps apply God's word to our hearts. It settles His words deeply into our soul and spirit.

Let's try this together. Fill in your name below.

_____, rejoice in our confident hope. Be patient in trouble, and keep on praying. When God's people are in need, _____, be ready to help them. Always be eager to practice hospitality (**Romans 12: 12-13**).

Now read the above scripture aloud with your name (it's more impactful hearing it out loud).

Does this change how powerful it is to hear your name in scripture? We pay attention when we hear our name.

Write out some more personalized scripture and meditate (read and think) on them this week.

You can purchase spiraled index cards and write down your personalized verses so that they are readily available to you.

*The key to personalizing scripture is to be intentional with your words and the posture of your heart. If you are thinking about other things, it will not be as powerful.

Date of session: _____

(Before session) List topics to discuss here:

....

....

....

....

....

Notes/summary from session:

....

....

....

....

....

....

....

....

....

....

My Homework:

....

....

....

....

Reflection After Session

What level of hope do I have that these issues will get resolved?

....

....

....

....

....

....

Did I feel heard in my counseling session?

....

....

....

....

....

....

....

Where am I placing God in my life and situation?

....

....

....

....

Use the following blank pages (14-16) to journal or draw your thoughts, feelings, prayers, or praises.

Two

I look up to the mountains—
does my help come from there?

My help comes from the Lord,
who made heaven and earth!

-Psalm 121:1-2

Spiritual Discipline #2

Devoted

Where do you focus your attention during the day? Social media, family, friends, work? Let's change that a bit. Learning to set aside time in your day to praise God by using **devotionals** is where our focus is this week.

Devotions help you focus on who God is, your devotion to Him, and His love for you.

Psalm 42:2 says: "I thirst for God, the living God. When can I go and stand before him?"

Wouldn't it be great to always have this hunger to connect to God?

Many times people who are hurting or struggling push God away. Maybe you can relate? While we are not promised an easy life, as Jesus told us in **John 16:33,** we are promised that God loves us and is always with us (**Romans 8:38-39**, **Hebrews 13:5**, and **Matthew 28:20**).

There are many types of devotions. I have included a few in the back of this book under "resources" (page 92).

As you are in counseling, know that God is with you. Always. Even if you feel unworthy or are angry with Him. God's love is not human.

God's love is perfect.

Date of session _____

(Before session) List topics to discuss here:

....

....

....

....

....

Notes/summary from session:

....

....

....

....

....

....

....

....

....

My Homework:

....

....

....

....

Reflection After Session

How can I apply what I learned this week?

....
....
....
....
....

What did I learn about myself?

....
....
....
....
....

How have I tried to turn to God for help?

....
....
....
....
....

Use the following blank pages (22-24) to journal or draw
your thoughts, feelings, prayers, or praises.

Three

For the mountains may move and the hills disappear, but even then my faithful love for you will remain. My covenant of blessing will never be broken," says the Lord, who has mercy on you.

-Isaiah 54:10

30 A.D Anyone?

Spiritual Discipline #3

30 A.D. Anyone?

I call this one **Living in the Scriptures.** Some scripture passages would be amazing to live in, such as the Last Supper, Psalm 23, or seeing Jesus after He rose from the dead. Some others will not be such as wars, stonings, and the crucifixion.

Living in the scriptures is when we read positive scripture and picture ourselves in the passage. When you do this, add sights and smells to your imagination to help the scripture come alive. This is similar to what movies and books do. They paint a picture that we can see ourselves in.

Try using an app that reads scripture to you. At this time a free app that does this is called Bible.is. Find Psalm 23 and listen to it. Use earphones if you can. See yourself walking with Jesus in a lush green valley next to a bubbling brook. Imagine Jesus is telling you to rest on the soft grass and drink from the cool refreshing water. Continue using your imagination by picturing yourself in this scene.

The beauty of using your mind with scripture is that it helps solidify the words of God into your heart. This is like reading a storybook with pictures. This method helps you memorize scripture to hide in your heart (**Psalm 119:11**).

Date of session _____

(Before session) List topics to discuss here:

....

....

....

....

....

Notes/summary from session:

....

....

....

....

....

....

....

....

....

My Homework:

....

....

....

....

Reflection After Session

What am I learning about my situation? Can I see it from a different point of view?

....
....
....
....
....
....

What are two areas I can give myself more grace?

....
....
....
....
....
....

Who is God to me and who am I to Him?

....
....
....
....

Use the following blank pages (30-32) to journal
or draw your thoughts, feelings, prayers or praises.

Four

I have come as a light to shine in this dark world, so that all who put their trust in me will no longer remain in the dark.

-John 12:46

No, Not That Kind of Hooey!

Spiritual Discipline #4

No, Not That Kind of Hooey!

The "M" word can get people all riled up. Meditation. Not the empty your mind kind of meditation hooey (which can invite dark powers), but the Biblical kind, of course!

Biblical meditation is all about focusing and filling up on the Word of God.

Why is meditation important? When we meditate on God, we learn more about Him. We discover His ways and show devotion to Him.

Philippians 4:8 tells us to meditate on beautiful, lovely, true, and noble things. All these thoughts bring us back to our focus on God who created everything.

Meditating on God's Word can help take our minds from darkness to light. From depression to joy. From loneliness to community.

Find a verse that stands out to you or one you want to memorize. You can even choose a scripture provided in this journal. Read it several times, write it out, sing it to a tune to help you remember it. Focus on this verse several times throughout your day.

Many people tend to meditate on destructive thoughts such as what they do not like about themselves or others. By switching the focus to meditating on God, your mood will be better and your relationship with God will begin flourish.

Date of session _____

(Before session) List topics to discuss here:

....

....

....

....

....

Notes/summary from session:

....

....

....

....

....

....

....

....

My Homework:

....

....

....

....

No, Not That Kind of Hooey!

Reflection After Session

What am I learning about myself?

....

....

....

....

....

Am I being open in counseling? Why/why not?

....

....

....

....

....

....

What are some things I learned about God recently?

....

....

....

....

....

....

Use the following blank pages (38-40) to journal
or draw your thoughts, feelings, prayers, or praises.

No, Not That Kind of Hooey!

No, Not That Kind of Hooey!

Five

So let us come boldly to the throne of our gracious God. There we will receive his mercy, and we will find grace to help us when we need it most.

-Hebrews 4:16

Spiritual Discipline #5

Lectio Who?

Lectio Divina (pronounced lexsho deveena) is Latin for "Divine Reading." Sounds fancy, right? It's a practice of meditation put into action by monks many years ago. This is considered contemplative prayer these days and is making a comeback.

This process helps connect us to God through scripture and helps us hear Him through His words. Isn't that the whole idea? Learning about God through scripture? This tool is one more way to do that.

Always start with prayer by asking the Holy Spirit, that lives in you, to guide your reading.

The four steps to this application are: Read, reflect, respond, and rest.

Read the passage up to four times. Notice what scripture jumps off the page to you. It may even be just a word or two.

Reflect: Repeat the words that are highlighted to you and ponder them. Ponder the understanding it brings to you.

Respond: By praising God for these words and revelations. Share your understanding of the scripture with God and what it means to you.

Rest: By allowing His words to soak in your soul. You can journal your revelation.

A great passage to get started with is **Matthew 11:28-30.**

Date of session _____

(Before session) List topics to discuss here:

....

....

....

....

....

Notes/summary from session:

....

....

....

....

....

....

....

....

....

My Homework:

....

....

....

....

Reflection After Session

How am I changing?

....

....

....

....

....

....

What is one thing that is helping my situation?

....

....

....

....

....

....

What is helping me feel comfort from Jesus?

....

....

....

....

Use the following blank pages (46-48) to journal
or draw your thoughts, feelings, prayers, or praises.

Six

All praise to God, the Father of our Lord Jesus Christ. God is our merciful Father and the source of all comfort.

-2 Corinthians 1:3

Borrow a Song

The book of Psalms are songs written by a few people. Scholars say that King David authored about half of the songs but the rest are attributed to Moses (Psalm 90), King Solomon (Psalm 72 and 127), Ethan and Heman (two wise people), the Sons of Korah, and Asaph (a chief musician appointed by King David).

We can identify with many of the Psalms since many share life's difficulties then asking for help (after praising God in the beginning). Other Psalms focus on praising God only. We can borrow these songs as our own prayers. I call this spiritual tool, **Praying through the Psalms.**

Using the Psalms as our prayers to cry out to God in our distress can be helpful in knowing how to pray. Locate a Psalm that identifies how you are feeling, then read that Psalm as a prayer to God.

For example, "Father in Heaven, as **Psalm 145** beautifully states, I exalt you, my God the King; I will praise your name forever and ever……"(finish reading the whole Psalm).

Even in our darkest circumstances, God is still the God to be praised and worshipped since we are not promised an easy life. God never changes and is always our rock and support, even in hard times. He is our life preserver when we feel like drowning. God sustains us, gives us comfort, and is generous with wisdom.

Date of session _____

(Before session) List topics to discuss here:

....

....

....

....

Notes/summary from session:

....

....

....

....

....

....

....

....

....

My Homework:

....

....

....

....

Reflection After Session

How can I apply what I learned this week?

....

....

....

....

....

....

Which spiritual discipline is working best for me so far?

....

....

....

....

....

....

....

How am I inviting God into my life and circumstances now?

....

....

....

....

....

Use the following blank pages (54-56) to journal
or draw your thoughts, feelings, prayers, or praises.

Seven

Let the message about Christ, in all its richness, fill your lives. Teach and counsel each other with all the wisdom he gives. Sing psalms and hymns and spiritual songs to God with thankful hearts.

-Colossians 3:16

Hum a Little Tune

*The Lord your God is with you, the Mighty Warrior who saves.
He will take great delight in you; in his love he will no longer
rebuke you, but will rejoice over you with singing.*

-Zephaniah 3:17

God sings over us! What a beautiful picture of our Heavenly Father caring for us.

King Saul needed David to play music to calm him down in **1 Samuel 16:23**. In **1 Chronicles 15:16**, King David directed his men to play music to worship God. Jesus and His disciples sang after the last supper as stated in **Mark 14:26**.

Music is our spiritual discipline this week. Music can help us worship God, see our identity as children of God, help us understand scripture, make us feel known, and uplift our hearts to God.

If you are in a dark season go listen to the words in **Glorious Day** by Passion. Right now.

Powerful, right?

Music is transformational and our help to move toward God/Jesus/Holy Spirit. Use music to help you feel connected and seen by Him. Pick your favorites and create a playlist.

Date of session _____

(Before session) List topics to discuss here:

....

....

....

....

....

Notes/summary from session:

....

....

....

....

....

....

....

....

....

My Homework:

....

....

....

....

Hum a Little Tune

Reflection After Session

What else is a sticking point for me?

....
....
....
....
....

Am I choosing to make needed changes in my life?

....
....
....
....
....

How am I scheduling time with God/what does it look like?

....
....
....
....
....

Use the following blank pages (62-64) to journal
or draw your thoughts, feelings, prayers, or praises.

Hum a Little Tune

Eight

Jesus replied, "I am the bread of life. Whoever comes to me will never be hungry again. Whoever believes in me will never be thirsty."

-John 6:35

Who Gives Us Our Bread?

Spiritual Discipline #8

Who Gives Us Our Bread?

Bread in the Bible is another word for the Word of God. Sometimes to really hear God well and get fed in deeper ways, we need to fast from food to receive fuller "bread" from God.

The Bible speaks on **fasting** throughout the Old and New Testaments. There are many reasons people fasted in the Bible including needing breakthrough, wisdom, casting out certain demons, ministering, repenting, humbleness, etc.

We learned from the book of Esther that, as a young woman, she needed wisdom from God and asked all the Jewish people around to fast with her. She was then given a plan on how to save her people.

Some people have medical issues and cannot fast from food. If that fits you, you can fast from things that are vices such as coffee, sugar, tv, etc. When you remove something that is a huge part of your life, you make more room for God *if* you focus your attention on Him.

Start with skipping a meal or two. Then incorporate some of the other spiritual disciplines we have covered such as Lectio Divina or personalizing scripture. Pursuing God is essential for receiving your "bread" when fasting.

Date of session _____

(Before session) List topics to discuss here:

....

....

....

....

....

Notes/summary from session:

....

....

....

....

....

....

....

....

....

....

....

My Homework:

....

....

....

....

Reflection After Session

What strengths do I have to help my situation?

....

....

....

....

....

What's one thing I can change to improve my life?

....

....

....

....

....

What verse(s) help me see God as my comforter?

....

....

....

....

....

Use the following blank pages (70-72) to journal
or draw your thoughts, feelings, prayers, or praises.

Who Gives Us Our Bread?

Who Gives Us Our Bread?

nine

"My sheep listen to my voice; I know them, and they follow me."

-Jesus (John 10:27)

Spiritual Discipline #1

Pay Attention

Pray. At the end of your prayer, ask God what He wants you to know for that day. Then listen. This is called **Listening Prayer**.

You may hear God in your thoughts or see a movie playing in your mind, or you may not at that moment. However, be on the lookout for other ways God speaks. It can be anything, even license plates and words on semi-trucks! When you notice something ask God, "Is that you? What do you want me to know?" Pay attention to those quiet thoughts. God's voice tends to be very subtle.

God speaks to us through scripture, nature, movies, people, or even in our minds by bringing us thoughts, words, pictures, movies, or sensations. God can speak to us in unlimited ways. God does not live in a box.

Have you ever had that experience where you needed wisdom and the thought of what to say or do came to you? That would be God.

Practice this tool of listening and paying attention this week. Don't get caught up in thinking things are a coincidence or ignoring signs. Take the stand that God is really speaking to you. If you struggle hearing God or knowing His voice look at resources on page 93.

Date of session _____

(Before session) List topics to discuss here:

....

....

....

....

....

Notes/summary from session:

....

....

....

....

....

....

....

....

My Homework:

....

....

....

....

Reflection After Session

Do I feel like the issue has been healed/resolved?

....
....
....
....
....

How am I feeling about myself?

....
....
....
....

What is making me feel closer to God?

....
....
....
....
....
....

Use the following blank pages (78-80) to journal
or draw your thoughts, feelings, prayers, or praises.

Ten

For I can do everything through Christ, who gives me strength.

-*Philippians* 4:13

Anglican Prayer What?

Spiritual Discipline #10

Anglican Prayer What?

Beads! **Anglican Prayer Beads.**

Prayer beads go back hundreds of years stemming from other cultures. In the Christian world, Catholic rosaries were developed first, and from that, Anglican prayer beads.

There is a huge difference in religious beads and symbolism within the beads, so make sure you get the correct ones for your purpose. Protestants (non-Catholics) will choose Anglican beads, which have thirty-three beads, representing the years Jesus walked on earth. There are 28 beads called "weeks" divided by four "cruciform" beads and an invitational bead.

The suggested use is to go to each bead with your prayers three times, which represents the Holy Trinity. You are using the beads as stopping points to pray and meditate on scripture.

Prayer beads are a great way to stay focused and use tactile sensations to engage your body in worshipping God. Using the beads is a great meditative tool to help you pray.

I highly suggest using a book with guided prayers to help get you started. Check out the resources on page 93 in this journal.

Date of session _____

(Before session) List topics to discuss:

....

....

....

....

....

Notes/summary from session:

....

....

....

....

....

....

....

....

....

My homework:

....

....

....

....

Reflection After Session

What am I hopeful for?

....

....

....

....

....

How can I stretch myself to step out of my comfort zone?

....

....

....

....

....

How can I turn to God for strength?

....

....

....

....

....

Use the following blank pages (86-88) to journal
or draw your thoughts, feelings, prayers, or praises.

Congratulations!

I am so proud of you. More importantly, I hope you are proud of yourself!

You took the time to care for yourself, get stronger, know God better, and love yourself so you can love others well. You learned new spiritual disciplines as well as discoveries about who you are as a child of God.

On the next page is your final assessment. Think about all you learned and processed as well as all the growing you did between your counseling sessions.

You may be done or just beginning. Either way, know that God is with you each step of the way.

For more support, head over to www.RedeemedHopeAz.com.

Bless you on your journey of healing!

End Self-Reflection

How has my life changed since beginning counseling?

....

....

....

....

How am I different since I began working on myself?

....

....

....

....

How has my relationship with God changed?

....

....

....

....

What spiritual tools were the most helpful?

....

....

....

....

Now What?

Ten counseling sessions may have been too much or not enough. Each one of us has our own journey which means that every person is unique and our counseling pace may be more or less than others.

If you are continuing counseling, you can refer back to the spiritual disciplines to nourish your soul with God. You can also start your own journal and borrow some of the questions in this book. Or you can purchase another similar book in this series.

I have created blank journals with the same cover for your convenience if you want to tackle it independently.

Bless you, dear one, on your journey to heal, be set free, and grow in your relationship with God, Jesus, and the Holy Spirit.

Amen!

Resources

All the resources I mentioned in this book can be found here.

Suicide Hotline:
988 (just 3 numbers)

Prayer Hotlines:
700 club 1-800-700-7000
HIS Prayer line:1-866-987-7729

Find a Counselor:
https://www.christiancounselordirectory.com
http://therapyforchristians.com
https://therapist.com
https://www.psychologytoday.com/us/therapists

You can also ask your larger local churches for referrals

Personalized scripture
Use spiralized index cards

Devotionals (suggestions)
Jesus Calling by Sarah Young
Strength for Each Day by Joyce Meyers
God Hears Her by Our Daily Bread

Listen to the Bible
Bible.is app (free)

Resources con't...

Meditations
Abide app
Soultime app

Lectio Divina
Meeting God in Scripture by Jan Johnson
The Art of Praying the Scriptures by John Paul Jackson
The Vine and the Branches Journal by All Things Bible
A Simple Pause (app)

Music (suggestions):
Glorious Day by Passion
The Blessing by Kari Jobe & Cody Carnes
Gratitude by Brandon Lake
Roar from Zion by Paul Wilbur

Pay Attention:
Communion with God Ministries: Hearing God's Voice

Anglican Prayer Beads
The Anglican Rosary book by Jenny Estes
Anglican Beads: On Etsy by Prayerbeadsetc.
Unspoken Elements.com

www.ingramcontent.com/pod-product-compliance
Lightning Source LLC
Chambersburg PA
CBHW051639120626
46551CB00014B/2141